Estoy Esperándote

A collection of poetry, Volume III

By Ayoka B.

AYOKA
Joyinhome Publishing

Estoy Esperándote

Ayoka B.

Published by Joyinhome Publishing

ISBN: 979-8-9897325-48

"What you want might make you cry. What you need might pass you by, if you don't catch it. And what you need ironically, will turn out what you want to be, if you just let it."

- When It Hurts So Bad, The Miseducation of Lauryn Hill

We all fumble and stumble in love. Many times, we haven't yet realized self-love which makes everything more difficult and sometimes, more painful.

When I was young, I didn't understand that self-love had to come first. This is not to say that I didn't love myself, however, I didn't truly know myself, not yet. Until you know yourself, you can not know what you need from someone else. And until you love yourself, you obviously cannot fully love another person.

For me, there was an added layer of daddy issues. The first man who was supposed to choose me and love me, did not. I didn't have an example of how I was to be treated and loved. I figured it out eventually, but after stumbling blindly. I recall a conversation with my sister. She said she used to marvel at the interactions of her dear friend Janet with *her* father; it was "foreign to her." She was in her mid-twenties when it dawned on her that their relationship was normal; the one we had with our father was not. At thirty-one, I finally let go of the anger when I acknowledged that I needed and *deserved* a father, just not the one I had.

This collection of poems describes the highs and lows of a love that is true, but neither of them truly knows themselves. And what can happen when you are ready and embrace the love that is meant to find you.

Relationships end. May you learn the lessons and heal.

Estoy esperándote

Estoy esperando para ti.

Estoy esperando para yo mismo.

Somos mismos.

Cuando terminas entonces empiezo.

Tus labios crearon para mios.

No necesito nada

No necesito nadie

Estoy esperándote.

Choices

I love that you choose me

Again and again.

First, you chose me as your dance partner

Winding and grinding in downtown DC

Amidst the crowd in the dark.

Then you chose me as your friend

And confidante.

Some have loved me, but seldom chose me

Even the one who should've loved me most.

Others could never follow through

Because they were broken.

Life is about love and choices;

The combination carves our path.

Thank you for choosing me.

I choose you too.

Everyday You

The curves that time has put on my hips
My extra thickness you love to tease with your lips
The way you listen intently
Or flowers out of the blue
Remind me why I fell in love with
Everyday You.

When you gaze at me in a way I've rarely seen
Again,
In that moment,
I know I am your queen.
Working overtime
Making sure the mortgage and tuition are paid and
Rubbing my womb when the cramps come in waves.
You hold my hand just to be in my space,
The look of orgasm etched on your face
Show me that your love is true
That's why I cherish
Everyday You.

You join in my silliness and we erupt in laughter

Shushing one another cuz it's waaaay after

Our children have fallen off to sleep

And tomorrow we have a schedule to keep.

I watch you kiss the baby and I quietly smile;

You embody the simple pleasures

That can not be bought

The basic lessons of life, love and loss

That can not be taught.

As we lay down,

I touch my cheek to yours and say,

"You make me love you everyday."

Writer's Block

You would think

Creativity erupts

When the turning points of our lives

Occur.

Death of your soul mate

The awkward, stumble into motherhood

Or the failure of love- the one God sent to you.

I stare at the blank sheet

And its emptiness

And wait,

Frustrate.

Weeks into months

Waiting for the insight

Or hindsight...

The remembrance of a moment that changed me.

That is worthy of the page

That will touch another heart.

Instead,

I am left to write

About the hole

In my soul,

That aches to be captured in word

But eludes me.

Naysayers

It may not be the perfect relationship

But he's perfect for me.

He ain't got degrees-

I've got enough for us both.

But, his tongue is a master of lyric and rhyme...

And these curves of mine.

I have all that I need

As long as I'm loving him

And he's loving me.

"It ain't been that long. How could love be that strong?"

"Three kids? Good luck," he said

With a smirk in his voice

And envy in his heart.

"Well what does he do?"

Tell me I'm beautiful.

"How much does he make?"

Enough to leave a single rose and love note at my door.

I have all that I need

As long as I'm loving him

And he's loving me.

Your Side of the Bed

I sleep

On the far side of the bed.

As if I expect you to slide in beside me

And curve your body

Around mine.

Others laid on that side,

In that spot

But could never claim it.

I lay awake staring into the darkness or slept fitfully

While someone was in your space, on your side

Until they left.

And so it remains empty

Cold.

Waiting for the shape of your body

Your smell,

To climb into the heavy covers.

I stay on my side out of habit.

Sometimes I stretch out

Determined to break the invisible barrier

But awaken on my side.

Only you can coax me back again.

Maybe then,

I'll rest soundly.

Screaming in Silence

I do not say things to hurt your feelings

Or to break your spirit.

In fact, I long to be the one

Who causes you to straighten your back and

Spread your shoulders with pride.

It's just that

At the end of the day

When the world has tried to best me

And I want to cry on your shoulder

You are not there

And I feel as if my heart might burst

From sadness.

The tears no longer well in my eyes

Because I have cried too many.

I am screaming

In silence;

Nobody hears my plea.

I open my mouth and my cries are soundless

To everyone

But

Me.

A loser at love,

My heart cannot handle another

Technical knock out

Least of all by you.

I try to believe in love

And will myself patience, but it is not my virtue.

Instead,

I am haunted by your scent

And flashes of what used to be

Or what could have been...

It is my love for you that elicits

Such fire and anger

When I feel you slipping from my grasp.

And I scream in silence.

I busy myself

To avoid the torment of what ifs

Or what may be.

A simple yet beautiful future for a family seems

Out of reach.

And she is unleashed,

Snarling and viciously protecting my heart from pain

As if it's possible

For my soul to bear any more.

Alone and glassy-eyed

I look at my sleeping children

And wish for a different tomorrow

That I might feel the joy

I see in their eyes everyday.

Why can't you hear me?

I didn't ask to be loved the wrong way.

I wanted to be loved the right way.

I wanted to

Laugh with you

Lay with you

Learn with you

Grow with you

Share with you

Pray with you

Stay with you...

Instead,

You loved me the wrong way.

You hid from me,

Lied to me,

Ignored me,

Betrayed me,

Left me.

But,

I didn't understand

And you never said

That you didn't know how

Because you were loved the wrong way.

Soulmates

I'm luckier than most,

I have had three soulmates.

One was killed by his best friend's nephew,

The next was running from unseen demons

The last one, I didn't see coming.

I'm luckier than most,

I have had three soulmates.

Although the first one was snatched before he got to

live, he changed my life.

We were young and loved hard, thinking we'd have

forever and a day to get it right.

I'm luckier than most,

I have had three soulmates.

But with him, time was never on our side.

The clock kept spinning and we thought

We would get in sync.

Life had other plans...

I'm luckier than most,

I've had three soulmates.

We had a long and deep friendship that

Spanned over decades, marriages and babies.

Our lives diverged and converged

Seamlessly,

As though we'd never been apart.

Haiku

Me duele alma

Esperando para ti

Espacio no llena.

Ayoka B. explores the themes of Womanhood, identity, love, loss and family through poetry, fiction and nonfiction. Her writing is vulnerable and honest which resonates with readers. Through her unique lens as a Black woman and DC native, Ayoka seeks to share the untold stories of mothers, sisters, daughters, friends and wives. Her goal is to help people gain clarity and insight into their lives.

Ayoka has a professional background in public relations and strategic communications. She received a bachelor's degree in Communications from Temple University in Philadelphia, Pa. and a master's degree in Public Communication from American University in Washington, DC. Ayoka is a mother and lives with her family in Costa Rica.

This is the third poetry collection in a series of four books. Her debut novel, *Love At Second Sight*, published in 2024. Learn more at linktr.ee/joyinhome